SOCIAL SKILLS BUNDLE

Leadership - NETWORKING

(BOOKS 1-2)

Nathan Smart

SOCIAL SKILLS BOUNDLE

Table of Contents

1. **Leadership**

2. **NETWORKING**

Nathan Smart

Leadership

Gain Confidence to Influence as a Leader Through Communication Skills and Coaching

Nathan Smart

© Copyright 2016 By Nathan Smart

All rights reserved.

In no way is it legal to reproduce, duplicate, or transmit any part of this document in either electronic means or in printed format. Recording of this publication is strictly prohibited and any storage of this document is not allowed unless with written permission from the publisher. All rights reserved.

The information provided herein is stated to be truthful and consistent, in that any liability, in terms of inattention or otherwise, by any usage or abuse of any policies, processes, or directions contained within is the solitary and utter responsibility of the recipient reader. Under no circumstances will any legal responsibility or blame be held against the publisher for any reparation, damages, or monetary loss due to the information herein, either directly or indirectly.

Respective authors own all copyrights not held by the publisher.

Legal Notice:

This book is copyright protected. This is only for personal use. You cannot amend, distribute, sell, use, quote or paraphrase any part or the content within this book without the consent of the author or copyright owner. Legal action will be pursued if this is breached.

Disclaimer Notice:

Please note the information contained within this document is for educational and entertainment purposes only. Every attempt has been made to provide accurate, up to date and reliable complete information. No warranties of any kind are expressed or implied. Readers acknowledge that the author is not engaging in the rendering of legal, financial, medical or professional advice.

Nathan Smart

By reading this document, the reader agrees that under no circumstances are we responsible for any losses, direct or indirect, which are incurred as a result of the use of information contained within this document, including, but not limited to, — errors, omissions, or inaccuracies.

Table of Contents

Page

Introduction..09

Chapter 1: Qualities Exhibited by Leaders............11

Chapter 2: Leading with Confidence....................21

Chapter 3: Communicating Effectively Before You Even Speak!..29

Chapter 4: Communicating Your Message With the Spoken and Written Word............................39

Chapter 5: Coaching Your Team to Realize Their True Potential...45

Conclusion..51

SOCIAL SKILLS BOUNDLE

Introduction

What is a leader? In its simplest form, a leader is someone who leads others – he (or she) may be a community leader, a political leader, a leader in the work place – there are all types of leaders, and that's where it can get confusing. A leader is not necessarily someone who is in charge, although the best leaders have an air of authority that sits naturally on their shoulders. A leader is, first and foremost, an inspiration to those he leads. You can be inspiring without having formal qualifications, but all the qualifications in the world won't make you an inspiration to others. A leader is a motivator, and the best leaders can encourage their teams to step out of their comfort zone to produce outstanding results on a consistent basis.

If all this sounds complicated, that's because it is. It's very difficult to define leadership, although you will know it when you see it. So, can anyone be a leader? Yes and no. Some people are born leaders, but leaders can be made too, and that is the aim of this book – to make you a leader, whatever your professional qualifications, life experiences or personality traits. The skills you need to be an effective leader can be learned, as long as you have the motivation to learn them and the wish to inspire others to perform to their best capabilities.

Good leadership starts with confidence – if you don't have confidence in yourself, you can hardly expect others to have confidence in you or in your abilities to lead the team. Then you need to channel this confidence into influencing others so they are happy to follow your lead. For this, you'll need excellent communication skills, and the ability to coach your followers so that they achieve what you expect of them. Leadership is not about issuing orders, it's about leading by example.

To be a good leader, you have to be someone worth following – someone others are happy to follow. That means you need to cultivate certain leadership skills, then channel them appropriately. This book will help you to build on the leadership skills you already have, and develop the ones you will need. You'll learn about the value of communication, coaching and leading by example. You will learn to listen as well as talk, to use encouragement rather than sanctions to get results, and to identify problems as they arise and deal with them without affecting productivity or denting morale.

The skills you will learn here will help you to stand out as a leader in any situation you find yourself in, whether it's professional, personal or anything else at all. You can become a leader wherever you are, whatever your situation. Just follow the advice in this book, and get ready to be a leader!

Chapter 1
Qualities Exhibited by Leaders

Leaders are not born to lead, but they can learn the skills that make them leaders. Kings may be born to rule, but that doesn't automatically equip them to be leaders, so birth and genetics have no bearing on whether or not someone can be a leader whom others will respect and follow. Certain life skills go towards creating a leader, and before moving on to the lessons this book will provide, take some time to take an inventory of your leadership skills and qualities, and work on your weak points as well as embellishing your strengths.

It's not about intelligence, charisma, or an imposing and attractive physique – although these things can't hurt and may help others to identify the leader in you. It's more about the kind of things that are difficult to recognize and quantify in others. These are the qualities that the best leaders exhibit. Work on them before you move on to the skills you will need to be an effective leader.

Integrity
Integrity is something everyone should strive for, but it's an essential quality in a leader, and if it's something you lack, you shouldn't even be reading this, because you, sir – or madam – are not leadership

material. What is integrity? People tend to think of it in a moral sense, but it's much more than that – it's a life choice.

At its heart, integrity means being true to yourself and your beliefs, whether they are personal, religious or professional, or a combination of all three. Your actions should always coincide with your beliefs, even when it might be more convenient to go against them, however briefly. Expediency should never win at the cost of ethics. Integrity fosters trust in colleagues and acquaintances, and if you aspire to leadership, you need to earn that trust, so that your followers will work with you and for you, even when things aren't going to plan. If they can see that you are consistent in your beliefs and actions, they will trust in your judgement and work with you to achieve your separate and collective goals.

If you have a set of standards guiding your actions, however basic, your dealings will be honest, and setbacks will be dealt with calmly. You will be able to moderate your own behavior, and ensure that your team does the same. People of integrity take responsibility when they need to, have the tough talks when it's necessary and deliver consistent results. People of integrity are leadership material.

Vision

Vision is a quality which is often associated with all sorts of people – not just leaders. Creative people such as writers, artists and musicians have vision, but leaders need to do something extra special with it. You have a vision of a particular project – how you see it developing, what needs to be accomplished to achieve the desired end result, how your team will work on it – and that's commendable, but it's only the start of the vision a true leader needs.

Having constructed your vision, and gotten fired up about it, you now need to communicate the vision to your team and infuse them with your enthusiasm and passion. That takes great communication skills, and we'll be looking at that later in the book, but before you can articulate your vision to your team, you need to own it, and make it yours. To do that, you have to look into the future – visualize the project, how you are going to begin it, how your team will be involved and how you will deal with setbacks. Vision is not rigid – it has to be adaptable to circumstances and amendable when necessary in order to stay true to what you want to achieve. Vision is action when you're a leader, and you'll need to recognize when it's necessary to step in and enthuse the team or change the game plan to achieve success.

Creative thinking

Anyone can be trained to do a task to a high standard, but when things go wrong, or when the game plan changes suddenly, it takes a leader to look for the best solution. It's a cliché, but thinking outside the box is one of the greatest assets a leader can bring to his team. A follower will say 'We've always done it this way,' but a leader will say, 'Why can't we do it another way?' Leaders are always on the lookout for better, more efficient, different ways to see through a project. They are always thinking, and their thinking is always creative. That's why a leader can take his team in a different direction when things get difficult – he's always looking ahead, and thinking of alternatives before they are even needed. Things happen to throw projects off course, but leaders will find ways to guide things back onto the right track.

Dedication

Often, the main difference between leaders and the pack that follows comes down to dedication. It's part of the package that makes a good leader. Being dedicated doesn't necessarily mean working around the clock, but it does mean staying focused on the goal, and being prepared to do whatever is necessary to achieve the desired result. That could mean working late, making an unexpected trip, having to bring someone new into the team because you need someone to take a fresh look, or even missing out on precious family time. True leaders are dedicated to the project, and to seeing it through successfully.

A leader will recognize what can be put off and what needs to be done to complete the project, and he'll help his team to see the difference too. It's a question of leading by example, because if you are not dedicated to your project, your team will soon pick up on it, and they won't be as committed as you need them to be. Work on your dedication skills on the small stuff, and it will come more naturally when the big projects arise.

Accountability

Ultimately, a leader is responsible for the successes – or failures – of his team. If he expects to enjoy the congratulations, he must also be prepared to accept the criticism when things don't go according to plan. A true leader doesn't blame setbacks on others – although if someone in the team has made a mistake he should be able to deal with the situation and any consequences in a calm manner and ensure that the same problem does not arise again.

Leaders make mistakes – in fact anybody who never made a mistake never made anything worthwhile – but they learn from them. They learn where things went wrong, and they learn how to deal with the problem. Most importantly, they recognize when to accept the praise, and when they need to take the blame. Leaders never blame others for their own shortcomings. They admit their faults, and improve on their performance, and this encourages the team to do the same, so that mistakes are quickly identified and dealt with.

Transparency

If a team is to respect its leader and work successfully with him, they need to know that, individually and collectively, they are trusted and valued members of the team. This can best be achieved by the leader's transparency. Without divulging sensitive information, the leader needs to keep his team in the picture on the projects they are working on. If the team don't know enough about the project, you can't expect them to channel all their efforts into its success. They need to be part of it all.

Transparency means being open to new ideas, and accepting that your way is not always the best way. Team members need to contribute ideas to validate their presence in the team, and feel valued for their contribution. Leaders need to listen with an open mind, and make a reasoned judgement based on facts rather than feelings. Whether ideas are accepted or rejected, always explain why a particular decision is made. This encourages the team to keep the ideas coming.

Always give credit where it's due – don't pass off contributions from the team as your own work or ideas. Ultimately, as team leader, you will get the accolades, but make sure your team members also get justified praise for their endeavors – and see that your colleagues and superiors know about it as well.

Assertiveness

Some people confuse assertiveness with aggression. Aggression is a negative quality which has no place in the skill set of a leader, because it's likely to alienate team members rather than inspire loyalty and co-operation. Being assertive means making your expectations clear, and communicating that while you understand it may not be easy to fulfil them, you nevertheless expect your team to carry out your discussions.

Being assertive means dealing with complaints and objections in a firm but fair manner, and it sometimes means having to say 'No' to a member of the team or a superior. Lack of assertiveness, or being aggressive rather than assertive, is one of the main weaknesses in leaders. Learn to recognize the difference. It helps if you can remain calm at all times, and other leadership qualities, plus the right communication skills, should help you to get the balance right.

Humility

Okay, you're a leader, but that doesn't mean you are a better person than anyone on your team – or anyone else for that matter. You are just a normal person with specific skills that mark you out as a leader. Recognizing this is important, because it will help you to inspire your team and bring out the best in them. If you are humble, you can let them know that they can also aspire to leadership. Don't go too far the other way and play down your position though. You got to be a leader because of your particular skills – it didn't happen by an accident of birth or stroke of fortune.

If you want an example from history of a great leader who was also humble, and inspired people to follow him, Ghandi is a perfect case in point. Non-violent, a person of integrity, transparency and humility, he changed the course of history. It doesn't matter whether you're leading a nation or a small team of workers in a project, humility will help you become a true leader of men – or women!

Sense of humor

A sense of humor is a great asset to have in any situation. If you've ever looked at personal ads, 'must have a good sense of humor' is one of the non-negotiables for a dating partner. For many, it's more important than traditional good looks.

When it comes to the work place and leadership qualities, a sense of humor is essential. It helps to foster a spirit of camaraderie between colleagues, and when the going gets tough, the ability to laugh at the situation – and yourself – can defuse tension and stress and restore harmony. Humor helps get you through the mundane, and gives your team a boost when they need it most. Be sure you laugh together though, and do not make a single person the butt of humor for no good reason. Read your team, and use humor accordingly, so you lighten the day but don't upset anyone. Used in the right way, humor can be a very powerful leadership tool.

These, then, are the basic qualities you will need if you are to be a successful, effective leader, whether you are in charge of a small team or a whole department or region. A leader should be a person of integrity, creative thinking and humor, who is humble enough to realize that he is no better than those he leads, yet confident enough to realize that he has something special that others are lacking. He should be transparent, accountable, assertive and dedicated.

Don't let this list of virtues scare you – most people have some or all of them instilled to some degree by their upbringing and training. What sets the leader apart is that he works on developing and improving those skills. A leader never settles for what he has – he always wants to be better, so that he can guide others to success.

Chapter 2
Leading with Confidence

Confidence in your own abilities – particularly when it comes to influencing and inspiring others – is an essential part of leadership. In order to communicate effectively, and coach others so they work effectively as part of your team to achieve your goals, you need to radiate confidence, even when you're feeling a little unsure of things.

Before you can inspire confidence in others, you need to be self-confident, and there's a thin line between self-confidence and arrogance. It's not a question of being so self-confident that you don't listen to criticism or you can't take on board your partner's or colleagues' advice and opinions – that smacks of insecurity. It's a question of knowing your own worth, and that comes from within yourself.

Confidence doesn't grow as a result of success – it's not dependent on external influences. However, without confidence, you will not make it as a leader, so it's something you need to work on if you aspire to be a leader. Leaders need confidence to make tough decisions and get their team behind them. Confidence allows you to make a decision and commit to it, even when the going gets tough. If your team can see that you believe in yourself, they will believe in you as well.

So, how can you build confidence in yourself? As was mentioned before, confidence is something that comes from within, so clearly it's to do with having the right mindset. These are some of the ways you can build confidence and become a leader.

Look and feel the part

Confidence is all about feeling good about yourself, and if you look good, you will feel good. So, dress smart, hold your head high and walk tall. Stride out, and step up your pace. Walk like you know where you're going, and like you have a purpose other than just getting from one place to another. Look and feel important, and you will be more confident.

Work out to tone up your muscles and increase your stamina, and if you need to lose a few pounds, get onto it. Exercise releases 'feel good' hormones into the blood stream, and it also helps you relax and sleep well. And if you look good, you will feel good, as well as projecting a good image to the people you are leading. Take control of your body, and look like a leader.

Keep the stress levels down, because stress will dent your confidence. You might want to try meditation or yoga to relax yourself and clear your mind of negative thoughts. Work on looking and feeling good, and your confidence will grow.

Practice and prepare

Don't leave things to chance, and don't make 'guesstimations.' If you're delivering an important speech or presentation, practice before the event. Run through everything in real time – read the speech, show the slides, cue the music – whatever you'll be doing, do it first without an audience. Then run it past somebody you can trust to give honest feedback.

Rather than read from your speech notes, print off using a large font, and highlight the main part of each section, so you can just glance down for reminders. If you're reading from a script you're not making eye contact with your audience. Eye contact is a sign of confidence, but reading from a script dents that confidence, because you come across as unsure of yourself and your audience.

Another thing that will give you confidence is to anticipate any questions the audience might ask and think about some answers to them. Research any facts and figures, and make notes of the things you think might come up on a separate sheet of paper from your speech notes. A little behind the scenes work like this will help you prepare and give you more confidence.

Always think past the actual speech or presentation. If any elements are controversial, have some arguments, statistics or study results available to back up your argument and answer challenges. Thorough preparation will help underline your authority in the topic and boost your confidence, so don't just 'wing it,' be well prepared.

Learn to give and receive compliments

Compliments are funny things. Everyone loves to receive them, and feels they should give them, but very few people can handle the art of compliment giving and receiving graciously. When someone gives you a compliment, just say 'Thank you,' and smile. It's enough. Most people's natural response is to be self-effacing in the face of a compliment, but all that does is demonstrate that you don't have confidence in your abilities.

As well as learning to accept compliments graciously, you should also make sure to praise someone who has done a good job. This shows that you notice and appreciate their contribution, as well as demonstrating that you are confident enough to acknowledge talent in others. A true leader celebrates the achievements of his team, rather than feeling threatened by them.

If you're sincere when handing out the compliments, you will win the support and loyalty of your team. Everyone likes to be appreciated – and a confident leader will let his team know that they are indeed appreciated.

Learn to accept criticism

The reverse side of the compliment coin is criticism. Nobody is perfect, and nobody gets everything right every time, so there will be times when you, or a member of your team, will be criticized. This is not a comment on your character, or anything personal at all. It just means there is room for improvement. Confident people listen to criticism and act on it – they don't try to justify their position, because they know that the criticism is deserved.

Most people realize when something has gone wrong, but some people can't cope with the criticism. They see it as a personal slight, or a reflection on themselves, rather than what it really is – an observation that something didn't work out according to plan, and an invitation to put things right. Be confident enough to embrace criticism, and you will make a great leader.

Don't fear failure

Failure gets a bad press, but it's actually something that everyone goes through at some stage. There's an old saying that 'Anyone who never made a mistake never made anything.' That should tell you that it's okay to fail. If you fear failure, you cannot possibly be confident of success. That fear will hold you back, so you need to look at failure in a different light. See it as a positive, rather than a negative.

Thomas Alva Edison, one of the most famous inventors and innovators in history, famously said 'I have not failed, I just found 10,000 ways that did not work.' He was confident that, eventually, he would succeed in what he was aiming to achieve. Take inspiration from Edison, and see failures as opportunities to extend your experience. Sometimes, you need to fail in order to gain new knowledge. While it's a good strategy to learn from the mistakes of others, sometimes you need to make those mistakes for yourself before you can move forward. Failure increases your knowledge and expands your skill set, making success more accessible.

Here's a third quotation for you: 'What doesn't kill you makes you stronger.' It's the same with failure. To be a confident, effective leader you also need to know what it feels like to fail. The first time it happens, it feels like the end of the world, but when the world keeps turning, and the sky doesn't fall in, you realize that failure isn't as bad as you expected it to be. It gets to a stage where failure holds no fears for you, and that's good news. It means you are more confident, and you can relay that confidence to your team by making it clear that although failure is not something to go looking for, nor is it something to fear.

It should be clear by now that confidence is not something you are born with – it's a state of mind that can take a while to become second nature. However, the good news is that just as the muscles in your body can be trained and sculpted to perfection, so your mind can be trained to be confident in everything you do. It's a belief in yourself borne of the knowledge that you can do – or be – anything at all. Confidence is what you need to be a leader – confidence in yourself, and confidence in your ability to encourage and inspire others. Once you have that confidence, you can work on your communication skills, but confidence is essential if you aspire to be a leader.

Chapter 3
Communicating Effectively Before You Even Speak!

What is communication? Put simply, it's the transference of ideas and information from one location to another through various methods – speech, writing and body language being the most obvious. Looks and gestures can communicate ideas as effectively as the spoken or written word. In some cases, what you don't say communicates far more than your words. However, effective communication is not nearly as simple as it sounds. It's not just a matter of passing a piece of information along and forgetting about it, it's a continual cycle of information exchange, understanding, interaction, and feedback.

If whatever you communicate is not understood, then the process grinds to a halt, because understanding facilitates interaction and feedback. Therefore, the initial aim of communication is understanding, whether you are communicating with one person or many, through the spoken or the written word. If you aspire to be an effective leader, you need to be an effective communicator. Fortunately, this is a skill that can be learned and perfected over time. Here are some of the things you need to concentrate on if you want to become an effective communicator, before you even open your mouth or pound the keyboard.

Learn to listen

Communication isn't just about you – it's a two way thing between you and your audience, whether it's one other person, several people, or thousands of people in an arena. A common mistake is to concentrate so much on getting your message across that you forget about the other half of the communication set up. You also need to learn to listen to the people you are communicating with. That doesn't mean just hearing the words they speak – pay attention to the tone and volume of their voice, note their expressions, take heed of their body language. Are they agitated, stressed, angry? Ask yourself why, and then ask yourself what you can do to ease the situation and improve communication.

There are several ways you can develop your listening skills, and it's a good idea to attend to this before working on your presentation and delivery skills. Experience 'the other side' first. Listen to people speaking, and engage with them. Work out what's good about their communication, and analyze the weaknesses in their delivery.

It's a communicator's job to engage his audience, and if you are not engaged as a listener, don't just switch off, ask yourself why you are not engaging with the speaker. This will help you develop your own communication skills, so it's an exercise well worth participating in. Remember communication isn't just about the speaking – there is non-verbal communication as well, and this can engage or alienate the listener just as effectively as the words the speaker uses. So, ask yourself what is preventing you from engaging in communication with the speaker. Is it what they are saying, or what they are not saying? Is there something in the tone of their voice, their body language, or even the way they are dressed that is putting up a barrier to communication? You need to know so that you don't make the same mistakes as a communicator, but first of all, concentrate on listening, because good communication works both ways.

Aspects of non-verbal communication

If you want to communicate effectively as a leader, you need to understand all aspects of communication. As has already been mentioned, listening is important, because communication is not a one way street. It's an interactive process. Too many people focus on getting the message across and forget that the way that message is received and understood is equally important.

Non-verbal communication gives clues to the audience and also affects the way they perceive you. You will have heard the expression 'First impressions count,' and if you want to communicate effectively, the first impression people get of you is important. Some people will have formed an opinion about you before you even open your mouth. It may not be fair, but it's the way of the world, and you have to go along with it. These are some of the ways you can nail non-verbal communication and give yourself the best possible chance of engaging successfully and productively with your team.

Dress appropriately

What you wear speaks volumes about you as a person before you even open your mouth. To be an efficient, respected leader, you need to convey that you are focused and in control, and ready to lead by example. That's not going to happen if you show up in jeans and a t-shirt, even if they're designer jeans, because jeans equals casual, and there should be nothing casual about your leadership style.

Dress to impress, but not to dazzle. You want your team to be intellectually drawn to you, as well as the message you are aiming to convey, so your clothes should be smart, functional, and tidy. Go for a suit or smart pants with a jacket. This works for ladies too, although they may prefer a dress or skirt. There's nothing wrong with that as long as it's smart, but don't make the mistake of wearing short skirts and flashing your legs in order to gain attention. You'll get attention alright, but it will be the wrong kind of attention, and in fact you will only succeed in diminishing your credibility as a leader if you use your physical attractiveness as a way of engaging with your team.

That goes for men too – don't rely on your charm to get attention, make full use of your communication skills. You're leading a team, not looking for a date. If this sounds like unnecessary advice, you'd be surprised how many people believe they need to be physically attractive in order for people to take notice of them. That's not the case, although some people are superficial enough to believe that only people who look good on the outside can be good leaders. That's the sort of thinking you'll come up against, and you need to be aware of it so you can counter it. So, dress smartly but comfortably – you don't want to be fiddling with bits of clothing while you're trying to communicate with your team. Be clean and tidy, and look like the competent and confident leader you are.

Body language speaks volumes!

If you want to be an effective leader, you need to be aware of your own body language, and also be able to read the non-verbal signals in others. That gives you a heads up as to how they are reacting to your communication skills, and it also provides a good insight into their attitude to yourself and fellow team members. There's so much around about body language these days that you can soon pick up all you need to know, but here's a quick guide which will get you started on body language interpretation.

As a leader, you want to come across as confident, focused and efficient, so your body language should be 'open' to display those traits even before you speak to anyone. To exude a confident persona, you should:

- **Walk tall**. Stand straight, with your shoulders back, and stride out purposefully. Don't hesitate, and don't shuffle along. Walk like you want to be noticed. Walk like you know what you're doing and you're in control.

- **Smile and look them in the eyes**. A bright smile, rather than a tentative lifting of the corners of the mouth is what you're looking for here. If smiling doesn't come naturally to you, try to remember a funny joke you just heard, or something cute your dog, cat – or your partner for that matter – did before you left home. That will always do the trick! Always, always, make eye contact with your team members. That's why you need the smile, because otherwise you could look as if you're staring aggressively, and that will put people on the defensive. People who maintain eye contact are perceived as confident, trustworthy and sincere – just like you!

- **Don't fidget**. Any movements or gestures you make with your hands and arms should look as if they're part of the presentation, and have a purpose. That's why it's important your clothes are comfortable – you don't want to be fiddling with buttons and fastenings, because it detracts from your authority in an insidious way. Try not to touch your hair, or your face, or your ears unless you are actually making a point. Think of your hands and arms as props for illustration purposes, and don't let them wander around unsupervised!

- **Speak low, but speak clear**. When you get to open your mouth, make sure it conveys the same impression that your appearance and body language have created. You are in charge, you are in control, you are confident. Don't mumble, speak clearly, and keep the pitch low. Yes, this is verbal communication, but it's following on closely from the body language, and reinforcing that first impression, so it merits a mention in this section.

Now you have a Body Language Blueprint to project the image of a confident leader. You can now look out for those same non-verbal signals in the members of your team. This will enable you to identify the confident ones, and those who are going to need a bit of encouragement, and maybe some coaxing and coaching to allow them to realize their true potential.

In addition to knowing how to read confidence from body language, you need to know how to spot the signals when someone is closing themselves off to your communication, and not engaging with you as you hope and expect. If a meeting or presentation is not going well, there will be indications from the body language of those who do not feel comfortable, and may even feel defensive in your presence. Recognizing these signs will allow you to change your tactics or work out a way to make the person or persons feel more comfortable and engaged with the message you are aiming to communicate.

- **Gestures are kept close to the body**. In the same way that controlled, open movements indicate confidence, if someone keeps their hands and arms close to their body – maybe even crossing their arms in front of them – they are not happy with the situation. This is a typical defensive, protective stance.

- **No eye contact**. Just as maintaining eye contact exudes confidence and openness, if someone avoids eye contact, it shows they are uncomfortable around you. Or they may have secrets to keep – after all, the eyes are said to be the 'windows of the soul.' If someone refuses to make eye contact, or if you cannot maintain eye contact with your team, it's a red flag for problems in the dynamics of your relationship, whether it's professional or personal.

- **Frozen face!** Okay, this is not a literal description, but when somebody is on the defensive, or if they are not engaging with you, facial expressions are kept to a minimum. No smiles, no raised eyebrows, no indications at all, because they have closed themselves off from you, and they don't want to let you into their space. You need to find out why this should be – it's part of your role as a leader.

- **Physical distance**. When someone is on the defensive, or is unhappy with how the communication is going, they will turn away from you, physically as well as intellectually and emotionally. This is most clearly demonstrated when someone turns their body away from you, even if they seem to be amicable in other speech and behavior. Instead of being open to your communication, they are closing themselves off from interaction with you, and you need to address this. Also, when you are in a negotiating situation and you are not happy with the way things are progressing, you need to be sure that you do not display defensive body language.

The body language patterns described above are defensive and uncomfortable, and someone displaying this behavior is not going to be open to communication or receptive to your ideas. Therefore, as a leader, you need to figure out why this should be. Is it something you are saying, or maybe the way you're communicating your message? If that's the case, you'll find that several people will be displaying defensive body language traits.

However, if it's just one person, maybe the problem is with them. It could be that they are not understanding your communication, or for some reason they are unable to feel comfortable with what is happening. Or maybe it's something entirely personal to them. Whatever it is, if you can identify these negative traits, you can at least try to make the situation more comfortable, for yourself and the team member or members concerned.

Being aware of the way you and those you work with communicate non-verbally, and understanding the significance of this interaction will help you to become a better communicator, whether you are interacting one-on-one or making a presentation to a crowd. The best communicators are those who can pick up on non-verbal signals and act on them so that their message is received, understood and auctioned, and all the members of the team are comfortable with it. It sounds like a challenging prospect, but actually a lot of it can be picked up by trusting your instincts and your experiences with others. If you can be ahead of the rest in understanding the significance of non-verbal communication, you will have a head start when it comes to what most people consider to be 'real' communication. Now it's time to see how your words can be tailored to motivate and inspire the members of your team to do what you want them to do and work together to achieve your objectives.

Chapter 4
Communicating Your Message with the Spoken and Written Word

As has already been discussed, communication isn't just about speaking and writing – there are other, non-verbal signals that you need to be aware of if you are to be an effective leader and communicator. That said, what you say or write is obviously of prime importance, because this is the measureable manner in which you will communicate with your team.

You don't have to be a natural at public speaking to be an effective communicator who can motivate and inspire others with his words. In fact, sometimes natural born orators can be at a disadvantage when communicating as a leader rather than a performer. Communication involves listening as well as speaking, and those who are used to speaking to an attentive audience don't necessarily make the best two way communicators, because they possibly haven't developed their listening skills, and they may not be able to read the non-verbal signals that are coming from the audience. So if you weren't the best in your year at school when it came to public speaking, don't assume that you will not be able to communicate effectively with your team. Here's how to get your message across when you're speaking to an audience.

Communicating through speech

Getting your message across verbally is something you're going to have to do on a regular basis as a leader, whether your team is small or large. In either situation, there are certain basic communication skills that will see you through, and they are skills you can learn, if you don't find they come naturally.

Be clear

Speak clearly, and make sure everyone can hear you. If you need to use a microphone, test it beforehand to make sure it's working properly. Once you begin to speak, you don't want the distractions of a messed up mic. And try to avoid stumbling over your words. Practice reading passages from a book, as if you were speaking to a room full of people. Make it a favorite book – one that you would love to share with others, because that's the nearest thing you have to your communications as a leader. You need to be able to inject enthusiasm into your presentations, because if you aren't fired up, you can't expect your team to be, can you?

Getting into the habit of reading and speaking out loud will help to eliminate unnecessary stumbles over words and the dreaded 'ums' that can stop your message getting across, or cause your audience to lose interest or allow their attention to stray to other things. It's a simple but effective hack to help you speak more clearly and engage your audience throughout the presentation.

Be concise

When you're communicating with your team, you are not entertaining them, although you will need to keep it interesting and motivating to engage and hold their attention. This is no time to show off your vocabulary, or your clever way with words. Save that for when you write the definitive book on how to be a successful leader! What you need now is clear, concise communication, with just the right amount of information and explanation to enable your team to understand the goals and carry out the tasks you expect of them with enthusiasm.

Put your thoughts down on paper to start with – the ideas you need to convey, the game plan, any problems that might arise, and the expected outcomes. Just a few sentences or key phrases will do. Now put together a presentation speech, and print off the first draft. Read it through, and score through any 'fluff' and padding in there – because there will be some! Now edit that out, and rephrase where you need to. Print off another copy, and read it out loud to pick up any repetitions, clumsy phrasing or superfluous comments. Make the final edits, and you should now have a concise presentation to deliver to your team.

Be polished

You've got the spiel, now here's the deal. Practice delivering your presentation. Time it, and be sure to allow plenty of time for questions and suggestions from the team. This is not a one man show, although you are the leader of the pack. Communication is a two way stream, and as well as getting your message across, you have to be sure it's understood, and that your team can ask questions, confirm details and make suggestions.

Spoken communication depends on getting the message across, and ensuring your team understand what you are saying, and what you expect from them. However, you shouldn't be talking all the time – factor in time for questions and suggestions, and be honest. If there is likely to be a problem, mention it, offer possible solutions and invite suggestions from the team. Ensure the communication flows, and does not simply emanate from you – it's two way traffic.

The written word

Everyone – with the exception of writers – prefers to communicate verbally. It's simpler, and it's more immediate. However, there are times when, as a leader, you need to communicate in writing, whether it's emails, reports, or writing a press release or an article for the company magazine. Again, it's a skill that can be learned, so don't stress about it.

The rules for effective written communication are pretty straightforward. Make sure your spelling and grammar is up to the task in hand, and check for typos. Anything that is sloppily written will undermine your authority and credibility, so use the spell check and grammar check, and back it up with a dictionary, because everyone knows that spell checkers are not perfect. It may be worth investing some time in an online grammar course, or joining a local English language evening course, depending on your abilities. It could save a lot of time and trouble in the future if you have problems with the written word.

Remember that in business communications, facts come first over opinions. You can offer solutions or suggestions if they are feasible, and informed guidance based on your qualifications and experience, but stick to the facts and statistics, and be honest about projected outcomes.

Keep emails friendly but professional, and if there are immediate or serious concerns, try to address them face to face rather than in an email. Sometimes you need to be on the spot to see what's happening, and your team need the assurance of being able to discuss problems and look for solutions in person rather than remotely. When there's a potentially stressful situation, it's easy to misread intentions in an email, but things can be made more clear in a meeting. As a leader, you need to know when the personal touch is needed to resolve issues.

Effective communication is something every leader needs to accomplish, whether that communication is verbal, non-verbal, written, or a combination of all three methods. By listening efficiently, picking up on non-verbal signals, preparing for presentations and polishing writing skills, anyone can learn to be an effective communicator. Leaders also need to know how to bring out the best in their team, so as well as being confident communicators, they also need to have coaching skills. The next chapter will show you how you can coach your team members and encourage them to stretch their capabilities to achieve personal and corporate goals with your guidance and leadership.

Chapter 5
Coaching Your Team to Realize Their True Potential

Having come this far, you should be a confident leader with effective communication skills. As a result, your team are motivated by your example and loyal to you. However, with the best will and inspiration in the world, some members of the team are going to fall short of your expectations – and their own. The spirit is willing, but they don't have the necessary skills, or maybe they don't fully understand their role in the team structure. That's when you need to step in and coach them so that they can fulfil your expectations and their own true potential.

Understand the difference between coaching and mentoring

Some people confuse mentoring with coaching, so be clear of the difference in your mind. Mentoring is something any competent member of the team can do for another, less experienced member. Mentoring is a higher level of training, but coaching is something different altogether. It's more customized, and tailored to the individual to bring out their particular skills, or enhance their abilities in a different direction.

Mentoring is more about on the job training and building general confidence and ability in the employee; coaching is about making full use of existing skills and taking the performance to a new level with specialized, individual training. The right coaching can empower employees, improving self confidence and interpersonal relationships, enhancing communication skills and boosting performance and productivity, which is, of course, the ultimate aim of coaching in a business environment.

Building on your coaching skills

Like most of the qualities associated with good leaders, coaching skills can be learned and improved on. Good coaches are made, not born. Many of the general leadership qualities will also help you to become an effective coach to your team. Confidence, self-esteem, communication skills and approachability are the main attributes which will ensure that both your team and yourself benefit from coaching sessions.

You also need to be adaptable, open to change and receptive to feedback, because coaching is not like teaching, although hopefully everyone learns from the experience – including the coach. Coaching is more flexible – you are not teaching from a fixed syllabus, although there will be a number of general principles and basic concepts that need to be communicated to those you are coaching. Above all, the coach should not be a problem solver – he should help team members to resolve their own issues by increasing their knowledge and understanding of the job and themselves.

The most effective way to build on your coaching skills is to understand why coaching is necessary, and what the expected outcomes should be. Is it just about team building, or are you trying to address issues within the team or the individual? Maybe the problem is higher up the chain of command? It's not always employee problems that create issues within the workplace. When you are clear on this, you can decide which of the various coaching strategies is necessary in particular situations.

Useful coaching tools

Coaching is a flexible discipline, and as such, you will need different tools in different coaching situations. These are some of the most useful, because they will cover most of the issues you need to deal with. As you become more proficient at coaching, you will develop your own methods, but understanding how to use these standard coaching tools will get you off to a good start.

- **Use statistics**. While coaching is individual, using data and statistics from current research and surveys can help you identify issues. You might wish to conduct an anonymous survey among your team, to gain some idea of their basic perceptions about the job, the work place, their colleagues and their superiors. Handled in the right way, this can be quite an eye opener, as well as providing valuable insights into how your team are thinking.

- **Use Assessments.** Used constructively, personality and behavioral tests can identify weaknesses and strengths in team members and provide you as a coach with insights into how to proceed. You'll get an idea of areas where the team member is likely to be acceptable to change, as well as flagging up the non-negotiables. We're talking properly formatted, scientifically researched assessments here – not fun quizzes lifted from Facebook, so choose your assessments with care, and devote plenty of time to analyzing the results.

- **Listen and offer constructive guidance.** Coaching is all about helping your team members to achieve their full potential so they can deliver the results you expect. Listen to their concerns, help them to differentiate between the important stuff and the things that can wait when they're under pressure, and lead them out of their comfort zone with advice and recommendations. You're not sanctioning against poor performance, your encouraging productivity.

- **Offer alternatives and solutions.** Coaching is a good way to empathize with your team members and find solutions to their concerns and issues at work, whether it's to do with the job itself, colleagues, management or something else. There may be personal problems that are affecting their performance at work, and coaching can help with alternatives. It's not counselling, but coaches need to be good listeners, and it may be that you can pick up on something that the team member doesn't see because he's too close to the situation.

These coaching tools will help you motivate and empower employees who are falling short of expectations in one area or more, but not every team member will benefit from or respond to coaching. Also, it's time consuming, and it's not guaranteed to get results, although various studies seem to indicate that coaching can often deliver better results than straightforward training, mentoring and disciplinary proceedings. Coaching helps members of the team who are falling short of expectations to analyze their performance and recognize where there are problems, before they formulate a plan to move forward and address issues. If you want to be an effective leader, you need to be an empathetic coach.

Conclusion

The theme of this book – and the main thing you should take from it – is that leaders are made, not born. Leadership skills can be learned, they are not instinctive, and they do not depend on any aspect or stage of your life. The young and the not so young can aspire to leadership, provided they can cultivate the necessary qualities,

Some of these attributes will be present in various forms, as a result of your upbringing, training and general personality traits. Leaders need to be confident and self-confident, but neither arrogant or self-effacing. Leaders should also be well versed in communication skills, and that means not just delivering your message, but making sure it is understood, and picking up on non-verbal signals from your team or your audience which may indicate a change of tactic or direction is called for.

Today's corporate environment places great value on coaching skills, and if you are to be an effective and successful leader, you need to add coaching to your skills set. Coaching is a step up from training – it's tailored to the individual, and aimed at realizing their full potential so they are able to resolve any performance, attitude or relationship issues and deliver the results you expect while growing in skills and personality.

Most of all, modern leaders are motivators and exemplars for their teams. They are not remote figures who command – and expect to receive – respect and adoration from their employees without doing anything to deserve it. The modern leader is right in there with his team, working for results, giving credit where it's due, and taking ultimate responsibility when things don't go to plan. He's accountable to his team and to his superiors, and he earns, rather than expects, their loyalty.

If all this sounds a tall order, and you are already ruling yourself out as a leader, take some time to read through this book again, and see how accessible those leadership skills are to anybody who wants to make a difference in the workplace and in the world. There is no magic formula to make a leader, and there is no set syllabus that qualifies you for leadership. If you can develop the right skills, and if you can motivate and inspire your team to produce the results you are looking for, then you are a leader, make no mistake about that!

NETWORKING

Learn How to Influence Others and Boost Your Social Skills. Career Growth, Jobs, Social Skills & Approach

Nathan Smart

© Copyright 2016 By Nathan Smart

All rights reserved.

In no way is it legal to reproduce, duplicate, or transmit any part of this document in either electronic means or in printed format. Recording of this publication is strictly prohibited and any storage of this document is not allowed unless with written permission from the publisher. All rights reserved.

The information provided herein is stated to be truthful and consistent, in that any liability, in terms of inattention or otherwise, by any usage or abuse of any policies, processes, or directions contained within is the solitary and utter responsibility of the recipient reader. Under no circumstances will any legal responsibility or blame be held against the publisher for any reparation, damages, or monetary loss due to the information herein, either directly or indirectly.

Respective authors own all copyrights not held by the publisher.

Legal Notice:

This book is copyright protected. This is only for personal use. You cannot amend, distribute, sell, use, quote or paraphrase any part or the content within this book without the consent of the author or copyright owner. Legal action will be pursued if this is breached.

Disclaimer Notice:

Please note the information contained within this document is for educational and entertainment purposes only. Every attempt has been made to provide accurate, up to date and reliable complete information. No warranties of any kind are expressed or implied. Readers acknowledge that the author is not engaging in the rendering of legal, financial, medical or professional advice.

Table of Contents

Page

Introduction...59
Chapter 1: Getting Down to Basics......................61
Chapter 2: Getting the Ball Rolling......................65
Chapter 3: Conversation; The Delicate Art...........71
Chapter 4: The Follow Up...................................75
Chapter 5: The Second Meeting..........................79
Chapter 6: Social Media and Blogging.................83
Conclusion...95

Introduction

Networking provides us with an invaluable tool with which to promote both ourselves and our companies. Whether you are trying to sell a product, a service or line yourself up for a new job this is the one skill you must have to forward your goals. Why do you think it is that eighty percent on top executive positions are filled without being advertised?

I think that most of us are aware, at least to a certain degree, how important it is to network in the modern day business environment and yet this remains one of the most underutilized weapons in our armory. Why? Because for many of us, engaging with strangers is difficult and uncomfortable. We would far rather sit in the security of our office banging out copy for brochures and press releases than actually take the bold step of going face to face with someone we have never met before. This despite the fact that deep down, we realize how many doors could be opened if we were just a little bolder.

Well here is something to take into consideration: very few people are confident in engaging with strangers, they have just learned the importance of stepping outside of their comfort zones. Sure some people are naturally so gregarious that they could approach a barn door and enter into conversation but for most of the others, getting out there and mixing demands a set of skills they have had to learn and develop. If others can foster these valuable skills then so can you and perhaps it's high time you did.

At their core, networking skills are interpersonal skills and that means that they extend beyond our work environment. Although we will look at most of the techniques we cover in this book from a business stand point, these methods translate into every walk of life where we interact with people. Understanding the needs of others and communicating those needs of our own in a way that makes them readily acceptable is more than just networking, it is an essential life skill.

Chapter 1
Getting Down to Basics

Where to network

In an age of technology and with an arsenal of social media resources like LinkedIn, Facebook and WhatsApp at our fingertips it might seem that the need for face to face networking has diminished, if not died altogether. Many of you, I am sure, are taking a great big sigh and thinking what a relief that is. What the experts will tell you, however, is that the need for interpersonal relationships are greater than they ever were and though these social media tools are useful accessories they simply lack the depth to create an initial connection with any substance to it.

The fact is we still need to get out there and make contacts and open the doors to communication. Just thinking of this probably gives you a knot in your stomach and even as you read this your mind is looking for ways to sidestep any such discomfort. Well here are two small items of good news: One, everyone else out there is as uncomfortable as you are and two, once you start to practice the skills set out in this book things will begin to get easier. I don't promise you it will ever be a walk in the park but with a little effort, one day you might be able to step confidently into a room of total strangers and make it look like it is.

Our network is all around us if we start to look. Obviously though, there are some environments that are more strategically advantageous to us than others and these are going to vary according to our specific business or career situations. Make sure to target the ones that will put you with the right people rather than those that will put you with people that are easier to talk to who but who offer little or no hope of advancing your cause. I say this because when venturing out of our comfort zones it is easy to choose the path of least resistance and then kid ourselves that because we are doing something we must be moving forward. If you are promoting the latest high tech computer software do not get into an hour long talk about it with the petrol attendant in the hope that he will run into somebody with a need for your product.

Many larger companies host charity events and fundraisers for various causes. These are great opportunities to meet people with similar business interests and needs to your own. Though these may have the appearance of social gatherings, when you scrape away the thin outer veneer, they are often networking events. The people organizing these sorts of functions are often desperate for reliable people to lengthen their guest lists for future events. Make sure you let it be known that you are interested and you can be sure you will start to receive regular invites. While you are about it, chat to the organizer and find out a little about them; it is most likely that they have a network that is quite impressive and if you let them know a little about yourself, you are suddenly networking already.

Sporting events and clubs are another area where plenty of business gets done and contacts get made. The beauty about networking and sport is that you immediately have an area of common interest and a relaxed atmosphere. They say that there is more business done on the golf course than there ever is round the board room table. If like me you have the capacity to aim a golf ball in one direction and then hit it in a different, and often surprising, direction altogether there are plenty of other sports out there. I ran for a social running club that was more about socializing than running but the contacts that I developed out of that were incredibly useful to my business.

For some people, sports events may simply be beyond the pale and the company might not be connected to any fund raising organizations. Well these are just two examples that spring to mind but there are plenty of others out there if you decide to look. Beyond that there are organizations that stage networking events and that takes any of the initial effort off of your hands. On the internet there are groups like Get Konnected but there are also companies that stage networking events that may be targeted to your specific product or profession and they will be more than happy to add your name to their next function list, though you might have to pay.

Chapter 2
Getting the Ball Rolling

OK So now you have chosen the event at which you are going to start your networking debut. You are now getting nervous, your palms are starting to sweat and you are desperately trying to conjure up a fever so you can shy off and not go.

Research

Instead of listening to your fears concentrate on doing something positive. Start by researching who is going to be there. If you are going to an organized function ask the organizer for a guest list in advance and don't by ashamed to ask the organizer who she recommends you try to talk to. Once you have targeted a few likely people with whom it would be good to make contact then hit the internet and find out as much about them and their companies as you can. Ask around and see if you can glean any advance information from your colleagues. What you are trying to do here is not spy on the person. You are looking for conversation handles and common ground that might make it easier to get them talking.

If your research does not throw up any information about the people you hope to network with then make sure you are up to date with a broad range of current events. What is going on in the world of sport, politics and within your industry are all conversation toeholds that will be useful to have. In many instances the first few minutes after an introduction awkward. If you have a few, easy to use, small conversation feeders, then you can take the tension out of that initial situation. What is more the very fact that you have relaxed the atmosphere will mean that you begin to be perceived as influential in the eyes of others.

Breaking the ice

For all of us this is probably the hardest part of any social interaction be it a networking event or a social gathering of some kind. If you step into a room filled with total strangers your natural instincts are defensive and you tend to make for the most out of the way corner from which you can observe whilst remaining as invisible as possible. In essence you are retreating to a cave.

Be aware that this is likely to be your first reaction and instead place yourself in a position where you can observe but where you are not hiding. This serves two purposes. It exposes you to others who may be in a similar position to yourself and may therefore approach you whilst at the same time allows you to look around and see who is the most approachable.

Studies reveal that people decide whether they like you or not within the first seven seconds of meeting you. This means that whether you decide to approach someone or are approached by somebody else you need to present a good impression. The impression you want to deliver is one of open approachability. Start off with a smile. Smiling is incredibly important at breaking down barriers. It says I am friendly and mean no harm. Whether someone approaches you or you approach first, offer a firm (not knuckle breaking handshake) and introduce yourself. Follow that up with some light conversation starters designed to elicit conversation. To do this ask an open ended question that requires a response of greater depth than a simple yes or no. Hopefully the person with whom you are talking will now begin to open up. If not have one or two follow up questions that are light and easy to turn into conversation.

Now the conversation has started, you have broken the ice and your next task is to be interesting. To be interesting is easy. We are all the most interesting people we know so if you can get the person with whom you are conversing to talk about themselves you will appear interesting without having given much more than your name. Listen attentively. This demands that we become active listeners and being an active listener is an invaluable skill to have. People like to talk about themselves but they need to be made to feel that what they have to say is of interest (even if it isn't). Maintain eye contact. There is nothing worse than talking to someone who is constantly glancing away to see who else in the room may be a better contact. For the moment whoever you are talking to is the most important person in the room. Nod in agreement from time to time and ask questions that will demonstrate that you are paying attention. Already you are smiling, relaxed and engaged in conversation and giving the appearance of being in control. You are starting to become a person that others are drawn to.

Let's not forget that your primary reason for putting yourself through this torturous event is to grow your network. Listen to the person with whom you have already engaged and make a mental note of any information that may be useful in continuing the conversation at a later date. Look for areas of commonality. These could be business interests, leisure activities or just having kids of the same sort of age. It doesn't matter. You are just mentally filing this for use at a later date. If you realize that there is no networking advantage to be gained through continuing this conversation then wait for an appropriate moment to make your excuses and politely slip away. The other person may offer no business development possibilities for you but their own fear of finding themselves alone in the room could mean that they are clinging to you just so they don't have to go it alone. You don't want to hurt any feelings here so at the right moment make your excuses and move onto another group or person to connect with.

Expanding the circle

Whether or not we make a useful contact on our first attempt it is a good idea to circulate and meet as many people as possible if your network is to grow. The procedures are the same with each now person you encounter but I would hope by now you have begun to develop a bit more confidence and further introductions are easier. By now you should have at least given the appearance of being relaxed and in control and you need to live up to your own image. In each new encounter ask questions, listen actively and look for areas of commonality. You will start to meet people with whom you know you can do further business. Continue to ask about themselves but throw in the odd bit of information about yourself and your own business or personal interests. Don't give away too much but offer enough tid bits that they can follow up on if they in return are interested. If they do start to take an interest in who you or your company are then be sure that you have definite and concise information that you can give quickly and easily. Don't go into a long monologue, just be precise and positive. This is the start up meeting aimed at opening doors. It is not the time to try to sell yourself hard or close a sale. A big word of warning here: Just as everyone else loves to talk about themselves so too do we. Talking about our own lives, goals and interests may be the most interesting thing we can do but it is not always quite as interesting to others. Don't fall into the trap of hogging the limelight. You may wake up the next day thinking what an interesting evening you had and then realize that you talked about nothing but yourself and learnt nothing about anyone else. Always keep in mind the primary goal is to expand your network.

Chapter 3
Conversation; The Delicate Art

We have touched on the early stages of conversation, the use of questions and breaking the ice but where do we go from there. At the heart of every relationship there lies a large element of conversation and networking is a somewhat of a business term for relationship. We have already touched on this subject in terms of listening skills and question asking but it is of such importance to what we are trying to do that I think it is important to dig deeper into what makes a good conversationalist. You cannot be a good networker if you don't have good conversational skills. It is that simple.

As we have already seen there are some pitfalls in the arena of conversation. One is our own to desire to talk about ourselves and voice our own opinions. We all have a natural desire to have our voices heard and if we want to network we do need to make some statements about who we are and what we are about. It is that delicate balancing act of getting information across whilst remaining interested in others that we need to look at closely here.

Whether we are relating one on one or participating in a group conversation there are certain rules we should try to follow. A good starting point is how you position yourself. When dealing one on one face the other person as squarely as possible and keep you body language open and relaxed. This makes it easier to be seen to listen actively and also to put in your own concise and thought out statements when the opportunity presents itself. In a group try to position yourself so that you are not pushed to the outer extremes from where you are less likely to be noticed and will have more difficulty being heard.

Once the conversation gets going I like to take on the role of active observer. In groups this can be particularly advantageous because group conversation is a bit of a battlefield with everyone anxious to jump in and have their say. By observing you will get a feel for who those are who genuinely have something important to offer and those who just like to make the most noise. Often they are not the same people. Also it may be that the person or people you need to network with the most are not the ones doing the talking. Once you have established who is who in the group then decide when would be an appropriate time to enter the conversation and bear in mind your talk time is going to be limited so be careful choose your words carefully. Don't forget to listen out for conversation handles at a later date when people you would like to network with are speaking.

In a group conversation you will often find one or two people on the peripheries who would like to say something but are drowned out or dominated by those more able to push themselves forward. Here is your chance to do something for the underdog that may pay off in the future. Invite them into the conversation and don't be afraid to do so quite overtly but cutting someone off and saying words to the effect that "I think that so and so has something to add to that". This little act of kindness demonstrates compassion on your part and that person will possibly be grateful enough to try to garner your opinion later. You never know. You may just be triggering a network opportunity without realizing it.

In group conversations, especially when they are in quite formal surroundings where not all the players are familiar with one another there can be sudden breaks in the conversation where everything goes deathly quiet and it all becomes a little stiff and embarrassing. Be prepared for this and have a question at your finger tips so that you can be seen to be the one who takes control and averts and awkward moment.

Your research and general knowledge will come into play now and you should have a number of light but interesting subjects that you can bring into use to keep conversation going. This very gentle oiling of the conversation along with your capacity to ask questions that lead to further conversation will subtly give you a position of control in these engagements and appearing to be in control makes you a more attractive person to network with.

Beware of those subjects that are controversial. You and the other members of the group will undoubtedly have subjects that you feel passionate about. Whilst passionate conversation and debate can make for a stimulating and enjoyable evening that is not what you are looking for on this occasion. Your job is to establish contacts and in this day and age where there is always somebody who is desperate to be offended about something controversy is not what you seek. In subjects that one is passionate about it is all too easy to lose control and give voice to your opinions and then drive yourself into defending them. In any other environment that would be fine but not in this one. On the other hand, if one of the other members of the group is foolish enough to voice a radical opinion it is a fine time to continue your subtle observations and see where the rest of the group stand and find who is passionate about what. It is all vital information to file away for a later date.

The same goes for humor. I recommend having some mild clean humor on standby. It can be an excellent tool for developing rapport. Bear in mind that there is usually someone who is the brunt of any joke. Once again you will need to be careful and err on the side of the politically correct. In general government and big institutions are widely acceptable targets but my favorite is to make jokes of which I am the fall guy. This way I am sure I won't cause any offence. By the same instance don't let anyone in the group start making fun of someone unable to defend themselves. There is no need to be rude but just try to steer the conversation in a different direction. Nobody likes a bully and though they might not have the courage to stand up to one, they will appreciate the fact that you do.

Chapter 4
The Follow Up

I really hope that by using these basic listening and questioning techniques you have not only developed your conversational skills but that you have begun to feel more comfortable with these situations that are so often awkward to start with. The good news is that the worst is over and whilst there is still much to be done, none of it will be as painful as that ice breaking first meeting. In large convention type scenarios things will start to settle down as the cocktails begin to flow and everyone has had a bit to of time to get to know one another and drop those masks they first entered the room with. Even in one on one meetings things should have moved on from small talk to things a little more pertinent to where you want them to be.

Continue with your gentle questions, always looking for handles but don't forget that these are mainly for use at a later date. Don't allow your questions to take on the appearance of an interrogation. Instead let them demonstrate that you are interested in the person or the people with who you are conversing. Now is the time to carefully start introducing a little information about yourself, your product or whatever else it is you are eventually hoping to promote. You are not trying to actually do any real promoting, just lay the ground work for a meeting at a later stage. Because you have listened so attentively to the other person you have created a situation in which they will hopefully feel obliged to listen to you.

This is known as reciprocity and it is an incredibly valuable networking tool that we shall visit again later in this book.

Having created some opening through which to set up further meetings it is time to start to think about moving on. You need to cast the net widely and not get tied into just one potential relationship before the gathering ends. The important thing here is to exchange business cards. If you can get some additional info like a Facebook address then that would be an added bonus. Always make sure that you have a ready supply of your own cards to give away on these occasions. If you get a few moments to jot some notes on the back of the card you are given that would be excellent though that is seldom possible on these occasions. Memorize as much information as possible and jot it down as soon as possible. Having a few details with the card you have battled so hard to get makes it a much more valuable prize when you next use it. Once you have exchanged cards and made tentative agreements about meeting soon then make a polite get away and start the process with another person or group. By the time you finally get to leave you will hopefully have a bunch of new cards and the start of a business network that will be invaluable.

The little pile of business cards you have acquired is of little relevance unless you act upon them. Don't assume that just because you gave away a pile of your cards you have now set the ball in motion for a network to grow. It is possible that your cards will be filed away in a card file with dozens of others and never seen again. Your treasure trove lies in the card you collected not the cards you gave away. It is important that you act on those cards within twenty four to forty eight hours while you are still fresh in the minds of those you met with. Like you they will have met with many people during the course of the last few days and you need to transform yourself from just another face in the crowd into someone that will be remembered.

A good first move is to transcribe all the short hand notes you jotted down on the cards into a broader format. Some of the information you gleaned will not have been written down and now is the time to store it while you can still remember which bits of information went with which cards. These days there are many formats for storing this information but I still like to write mine down in good old not form logging the date of meeting, where it took place and any further relevant intelligence I might have gathered. Once I have all that information logged I can go through it and prioritize anything that needs to be acted on before the rest. For example, I may have heard the Bob's wife was having an operation today. I could drop him a quick e mail along the lines of "Hi Bob. My name is …. and we met at the function last night. You mentioned that your wife is having an operation today and I just wanted to say that I hope it all goes well." It sounds like a small thing but it places you in Bob's mind for a second time and demonstrates that you paid attention to what he had to say. Obviously this is just an example but I hope it shows how the network has started to develop and what value small seemingly unimportant pieces of information can be valuable.

In many cases you will not have gained such a useful handle but you can still send a follow up email stating how glad you were to have met the night before and mentioning that you hope to get together again soon. If there was an obvious opening to further meetings then you can ask for an appointment immediately but if things were less clear then content yourself with just a quick note designed to establish yourself in that other person's memory. This is a judgement call that only you can make relative to your unique circumstances but do be careful about coming on too strong even if you are eager to progress the relationship. Most relationships take time to mature and rushing forward may make you appear either too pushy of desperate. Often the person you have targeted to build into your network is more established than you are and he may be a little less keen to move things forward. Take your time and move cautiously. The door has to be opened rather than knocked down.

Chapter 5
The Second Meeting

If you are lucky you will have established that there is some sort of synergy right from the start and you are able to set up a meeting on that first follow up call. If not use the follow up call to establish yourself in their memory and then a few days later try to set up that vital second meeting. In many ways the second meeting uses similar techniques to the first but now the ice has been broken and you can be a little more proactive about presenting yourself. You still need to ask questions and use your active listening skills but now you can participate more in the conversation though it is always best to allow the other party to do most of the talking. A one third talking to two thirds listening ration seems to work quite well. You should differentiate between network building and marketing meetings. Even if selling a product or selling yourself is your long term aim, building that vital network should still be the priority and all too often we derail this with our desire to rush to the end goal without laying the necessary groundwork. In the short term you may be able to push forward and elicit a sale but with a longer term approach you could develop a relationship that opens the door to many sales.

Continue to look for handles to use at a later date. Look for areas of need that the other person has and then see if you can fill them in some way. For example, during the meeting he may mention that he is looking for a certain piece of equipment. If in a few days time you are able to locate something that his needs it gives you an excuse to make contact yet again. Better still it now creates a degree of indebtedness. Studies have revealed that people do not like to be indebted and so they are inclined to do something in return to eliminate that feeling. This is known as reciprocity and at first it may sound quite mercenary but what you are doing is looking for a need, filling that need and then having someone reciprocate by filling a need you may have.

Networking is an ongoing process and you need to constantly bear in mind that you must keep developing and fostering relationship in order to build on it. Your second meeting will hopefully lead to a third and so on. If things develop the way they should you will find yourself being invited into new circles that may not have been available to you before or which you may not even have considered. The overlap between one circle and the next does not really matter even if it is small. As you develop different circles so you will have contacts that may be of use in different ways. To go back to the last example and the piece of equipment you needed to find. Perhaps you knew someone in a completely different circle and thus were able to locate a source for the equipment needed. By tapping into contacts from the one circle you are able to use that to open a completely different circle.

Finally, don't be possessive of your contacts. Some people are mean spirited with contacts and hope that hiding one from the other they will benefit by being the middle man. In fact, the opposite is nearer the truth. If you have two contacts and you know that one could benefit from meeting the other then offer to put them together. Once again that simple piece of generosity that cost you nothing

Nathan Smart

will engender reciprocity and may lead to your being paid back with interest.

Chapter 6
Social Media and Blogging

Twenty years ago the need to discuss social media in the field of networking would have been unnecessary. Today it is hardly possible to bring up the one subject without incorporating the other. Social media has become the go to tool for everyone from company executives to pop starts. Even politicians all now have web sites and twitter accounts. As a tool they can be highly effective at bringing us into contact with people we might want to connect with. The problem is, many people have begun to use these tools exclusively and I prefer to treat them as tools that enhance networking skills rather than tools that replace them. I have deliberately placed them further into the text of this book because I think that they are not as important or as useful as face to face meetings and they still require a certain amount of tact and diplomacy in their use. Many of the skills we have already dealt with are translatable, either directly or indirectly, to the social media field.

There are of course dozens, if not more, different platforms that can be used for networking. I will be dealing with the three main ones which are Twitter, Facebook and LinkedIn. Right up front it is important to emphasize that if you are networking for the purposes of business then you need to stick to business in that area of whichever platform, or platforms, you choose to use. If you have a Facebook account that you use to contact family and friends and for sharing your latest batch of photographs then keep it to family and friends and don't bring your business associations into it. Your networking clients do not need to see the pics of your dog eating a watermelon and you certainly don't want them seeing you with too many beers down your neck dressed in your wife's bathrobe with a shower cap on your head. If you have an account of this type then keep it private though I would go one step further and warn you always to be very discerning about anything you put on the internet no matter what capacity it is in. (Clearly most of the world disagree with me on this particular subject)

The platform of preference for most business dealings seems to be LinkedIn. Although both Twitter and Facebook offer great possibilities in the business arena, LinkedIn is the main place that business type networking takes place. For that reason, I will start with LinkedIn and then take a shorter look at the other two. As I mentioned there are also many others which can still be very effective but they tend to be more specific to certain professions or groups of user.

LinkedIn

There are many books and sites that will give in depth information on the different ways to use this platform but I will deal with some general points that are most important. The first thing you have to consider is your personal profile and that may not be as easy as it appears. You really want to sit down and think what I am I trying to portray here and what are the most unique and positive aspects about me that will best serve that image. Are you selling yourself and your personal skills or are you presenting a product or service? I believe that what you are presenting first and foremost is your own character. Anything else that you are offering is secondary to who you are and the qualities that you offer. You are not Bob Smith, purveyor of fine pumps that have been manufactured for the last one hundred and fifty years and that come with a lifetime guarantee. You are Bob Smith, qualified and reliable marketing person with years of experience in the sales industry and a deep appreciation of customer needs. Oh and by the way at the moment you are selling these fine pumps. Networking, whether face to face or on social media platforms, is about who you are. People are not looking to build a relationship with a product; they are building a relationship with you. You are the networker.

The first few lines of your profile are the most crucial. All the rest, including qualifications and experience are very important but it is those first one or two sentences that may be your only chance of standing out from the crowd. I suggest you write out a profile and then sleep on it for the night and check it again in the morning before you post it.

Once you have a profile up and running you need to think about who you are going to attempt to link to and how you are going to go about that. Here is where you go back to your notes collected from the networking functions and you then filter out any that you may not feel would work for you on this particular platform. Once you have a selected target group it is time to search the platform and see if they are listed and then put in a connection request. Don't just send out a generic note saying Hi I would like to add you to my connections. You have some personal details you can include in your invitation and you may need to remind the person where you met and anything else that seems pertinent to connecting with them.

Fairly quickly and painlessly you will start to grow your network. You will also find that people will start to approach you to link up to their network. There are two differing schools of thought here. One is that you should have as many connections as possible and the other that you should keep your connections to people you have a definite affiliation with. The first school of thought is based on the principal that if you have thousands of connections you have a greater possibility of finding some sort of common interest with them. The second is that you can have a more in depth relationship with fewer key players and that those with thousands of connections are unable to follow them closely anyway. There is no right or wrong answer here. For some people the numbers game may play more in their favor whilst for others a tighter more targeted approach may be most beneficial. That will be best decided by you in terms of your own goals and objectives.

Whichever route you choose the rules are the same. Pay attention to what others have to say and make sure that whatever you say has value and is interesting. When your comments pop up on the screen you want people to feel that they must take a second look.

In networking terms, the big plus of LinkedIn is that is gives you a look at your connections contacts and there may well be people there that you want to reach out to. The best route is to go via your connection and give a brief explanation as to what mutual benefit there would be to his contact and yourself if he were to introduce you. People don't like to make introductions if their contact is then going to be bombarded with marketing pitches. If you present a logical and reasonable case for the introduction to be made then you overcome this resistance and the connection being approached will be much more willing to establish contact. As always in the network building game the way to move forward is slowly and gently.

One of the great upsides to LinkedIn is its groups and if you are building a network and want to establish your credibility this is the place to be. Groups enables you to target special interest areas that are pertinent to you. By following the various discussions you will get to know who the main players are and what their feeling is on certain subjects. Watch for a while and then start to participate and give positive feedback and input to their articles. Eventually you may have made enough of an impression to connect with them. At the very least you will have some insight into the way they think and what they are up to.

This is also the area where you will be able to post your own comments and start to be seen as a player in the field. You have some time here so make sure any comments are well thought out and researched and that you can back up what you have to say. Soon you will start to develop a following of your own and in general the groups tend to be like minded people who are quite supportive. There will, however, be those who are contrary often for no other reason than that they can be. The internet provides a voice for some who just want to be seen to have an opinion that is different. I suspect many of these mean spirited folk are the same sort that would not say boo to a mouse in the face to face world but now they can enter the fray from the shelter of their living room and give vent to their opinions. Be very careful how you deal with these situations. Present you argument clearly and politely and then step back. Often others following the discussion will step in and engage on your behalf. Your position now becomes one of observer. In depth social media rows will not help build your network.

Twitter

With just one hundred and forty characters to build a following, Twitter took some time to get my head around at first but has gone on to be my most useful social media tool. The one thing about this platform is that you soon learn that the world is packed full of people who want to say something even when they have nothing to say. I have not gone down the route of having thousands of followers just so I can say that I have them. I have tried to be really selective about who I follow yet still my time line is often littered with people who make the mistake of thinking that I really care what they had for breakfast. Twitter is excellent for gathering information fast. If you are following experts on certain subjects you very quickly see what they want to say and click to the articles that they normally attach to their tweets. It does not take long to work out who the movers and shakers are in your field and separate them from those that simply generate white noise. You have the option of creating lists and you can then put the people who really interest you in to those categories you have created. This enables you to make very quick assessments of what is happening at any given time on a given subject.

There is a certain etiquette to using Twitter which many people don't seem to grasp but which still remains important to the network builder. For starters this is not a communication tool like SMS. Twitter offers a perfectly effective direct message system to contact a person privately so there is no need to share with all you followers that you will be arriving at the restaurant in fifteen minutes and could the person you are meeting please order you a Martini. It is also important to be selective in what you tweet and only tweet material that is genuinely interesting to a large audience. If someone hogs the time line with a series of inane tweets, I immediately mute them. The ultimate compliment is to retweet somebody else's tweet but just as with your own tweets don't retweet inane comments purely in the hope of being followed by someone you would like to be connected to. Be considerate to all those followers and retweet material that is interesting and informative. You are trying to establish your own credentials so though you may be generous in retweeting bare in mind that people are following you because they want to know what you have to say so make sure you put up some interesting material of your own.

Twitter is a platform that really draws the trolls out of the woodwork. These nasty little people, for whom the word troll is ideally suited, love to attack people with contrary opinions. As with Facebook, the best way to deal with them is to step away and not engage which only feeds their frenzied minds. I prefer not to use this platform as a place to air really controversial views. Controversy does not work for me but for others it may be a tool that works in their favor though they need to be fairly brave.

Whilst there is no doubt that this platform has great potential to increase the size of your network I would like to end with one word of warning. Twitter along with all the other social networking platforms can be quite addictive and demanding of your time. It is easy to get carried away with reading tweets and creating tweets of your own but always ask yourself if what you are doing is being really constructive or if it is simply absorbing time that might be better used elsewhere.

Facebook

I have left the big daddy of social media platforms until last. I suspect that most people are now aware of this platform and how it works because it is so widely used on a private basis. Even if you have been using Facebook for yours to communicate with friends and family you need to remember that using it for network building is going to be totally different. Because you should not be muddling your network building affairs and your more personal life you will probably need to open a new page specific to the network you are building. Not only will you need to be careful what you put up on that page, you will also need to be circumspect as to who you invite into your circle because if somebody posts material that is not suitable to your image in some way or other you risk being associated with whatever it is they put up.

All the warnings aside this is still a great network building platform. Like the other two mentioned there are some rules you need to follow. You should be updating at least once or twice a day if you want to develop and maintain a high profile. Research shows that less than one third of Facebook users log in every day and another third once or twice per week. Consistency will therefore make you more noticeable.

Create content that encourages people to engage with you. Just like in the face to face meetings, start asking questions if you want to develop a conversation. Also when you are left a question make sure you reply. As with Twitter joining a few groups that are relevant to what you are trying to achieve and once you have observed for a while dive in and participate. You will soon discover that participating in group conversations regularly soon elevates your profile.

Be careful not to over comment and always be polite and tolerant of others.

There are differing times when sites are most active and so by observing these you can start to be tactical about when you post your comments. Most people tend to be active of Facebook in the afternoon and then there is another rush in the evenings which is often occurring on portable devices. This will vary if for example you are approaching the platform from the East to the West coast of the US or the US from Europe. That may all seem a bit confusing at first but you will soon get the hang of it simply but watching when other posts are put up.

To increase your network you will need to be constantly inviting new contacts into your circle. Facebook has great tools for finding contacts and the groups themselves are a wonderful method of reaching people you have already qualified as being interested in similar topics to those you are interested in.

One thing about both Facebook and Linked in is that they provide great reminders of things such as birthdays and change in working circumstances that become handles to say a quick hello.

All three of these platforms are so socially acceptable nowadays that they have transformed how we network. Interestingly though, the rules that were first developed in the face to face relationship area remain exactly the same only now you are able to network on a far larger scale. Those basics of common courtesy are still very applicable even if some choose not to use them. Listening to others and giving in order to get are intrinsic to any relationship building exercise.

To blog or not to blog

The choice to start you own blog or not is one you should consider carefully. I don't intend to tell you how to blog but we can take a brief look at some of the pros and cons in relation to your networking objectives.

Starting a blog definitely went through some fundamental changes in the last decade or so and it is now so easy that the average school kid can put one together. To make your blog stand out from the crowd and give a generally professional image may be a little more complicated and the time this entails will need to be weighed up. Of course if you have the money it need not be too very expensive to get a professional to build a site to your specifications. Whether you build it yourself or you hire in outside help make sure that the final product portrays you as competent.

Once you have your web site built you are ready to start providing content. The beauty about this is instead of now being reliant on other people to discuss the subjects that interest you or portray your project well, you can do this yourself. Once you publish you can link it through to your other social platforms or putting it up in the various groups you have joined. Not only do you control and create your own material you also have the option of using the tool as a handle in itself. For example, you can approach an expert in your field and ask if he would mind writing a guest blog or doing an interview. In networking terms this may be a tool too great not to use.

There are some down sides though. You have your blog up and running, you are writing content and developing a following and most importantly you are now master of your own destiny as far as material is concerned. The problem is that maintaining a blog is time consuming. You need to think of fresh content at least once a week and then you need to be a good enough wordsmith to put it together and technical enough to put in some photos or other media. After that if you start to gain traction you will start gathering followers who will leave comments and those will require replies. You may think you have miles of material to create some interesting posts, but do you have enough to do so week after week as well as run the rest of what goes to making up your life?

Overall if you are sure you can put together a blog and keep on top of all that running it well entails then I would say go for it. It certainly gives you much more freedom in generating content and if you can make it interesting you will gather followers and boost your network. I suggest writing out a fairly comprehensive list of content and providing you are sure you have enough articles buzzing around in your head to put together at least enough for a new weekly post every week for the first month or two then this is a powerful medium. Research the whole blogging subject well before you start and make sure you only put it out there if you can do it justice and it can do the same for you.

Conclusion

In essence, networking is about building relationships. Whether you want to do this from a business point of view or simply to expand your social life the skills required are the same. Social media platforms may have changed how we present this but don't be fooled; traditional values, manners and kindness are as valuable on dating sites, business network platforms or straight face to face meetings as they ever were. Much of what you have read here should be almost instinctive. The sort of thing your mother drummed into your head when you were a kid. Sadly, we live in a world where so much of this basic stuff has just been forgotten or pushed aside in the day to day rat race we call life.

Paying attention to other people, listening to them and showing interest in what makes them tick and offering help when you can provide it are not just networking skills. These are just the threads woven into the fabric of being a decent human being. The tools may have changed and evolved. The principals are timeless.

Nathan Smart

SOCIAL SKILLS BOUNDLE

www.ingramcontent.com/pod-product-compliance
Lightning Source LLC
Chambersburg PA
CBHW061150180526
45170CB00002B/712